This book is from:

_____

To you

_____

Bark: A Series

Tale of a Tail on a Forest Trail

BY MEGHANN TIMMS

Illustrations by Kenn Yapsangco

Copyright © 2014 by Meghann Timms.

All rights reserved. No part of this book may
be reproduced or transmitted in any form or by
any means, electronic or mechanical, including
photocopying, recording, or by any information storage
and retrieval system, without permission in writing from
the copyright owner.

Print information available on the last page.

Bark: A Series

Tale of a Tail on a Forest Trail

Waiting and watching the hands on the clock, Bon Bon couldn't wait to go for her walk.

Out the front door into fresh mountain air.
Wait-what's that *smell?* Time to stop and stare!

Deer on the grass, munching away,
Bon Bon couldn't believe! Did they want to play?

Yipping and yapping, she approached them all, Yipping and yapping, "would you like to play ball?"

The deer were so startled at the sound of her yip, In the other direction, they started to skip.

No wait! Come back! Please don't go away!
Bon Bon *ran* to them,
yipping, "please stay-stay
and play!"

But the deer didn't hear, didn't seem to care,
Off through the thicket, through the dark forest air.

Sounds of hard hooves clopping pine needles and dirt, Ooh! Ouch! Bon Bon's paws *really* hurt!

Stopping and panting, tired and sore, Chasing deer was no fun-this was such a chore!

Turning 'round, ready to head back,
Whoa, wait a minute...which direction *was* that?

Alone and shivering in the cold winter air, Bon Bon started to panic- panic and despair.

Until-wait! Yes, she heard it, a familiar sound.
Bon Bon's face lit up, wildly looking around.

Galloping, galloping, as fast as she could,
Feverishly tearing through the dark, dusky wood.

Back over the lawn, 'til she could finally see, Her tail set a waggin'- there was her family!

Bon Bon was happy, *so* happy, back at home,
Never *again* from her house would she roam!

www.ingramcontent.com/pod-product-compliance
Lightning Source LLC
Chambersburg PA
CBHW050753110526
44592CB00002B/48